Thank You...

We would not have met if it hadn't been for

Then there

a way of surprising

when I least expect it.

The last time this happened was

Our best times have been

Absolutely love you!

impulsive nature.

I remember the time I was so surprised when you

One time when I especially needed you was

To cherish the times
we have had and the

I can't wait until we

both know is a gift.

Thank you for

Remember the first time we

Thanks for

being so patient

Some day, I hope we will be able to

I'll always remember

I cherish the moments we

Your best qualities are

The days

go by

Thanks for always remembering

All I need is you and

the life we have together.

Without you I was

Thank you for

My wish for you is

Thank You

Our love grows with each moment. I see this every day as

Cheers to us!

Thanks for the

Remember how we celebrated

Thank You
for your [illegible]

in all circumstances.

Did you know that I can always depend on you for

Thanks

for keeping

I love surprises, especially like the time that you

Thank You

We've shared so many special times with our friends like this one

Thank You
Enjoy

sweet and savory.

Whether it's in the kitchen, or elsewhere, we both love to eat

I am grateful for being

Thank you for

Thank You

moments with me.

I like to remember this small anniversary of ours

Our travels together have included a few surprises

Thank You

moments you have given me.

Our lasting love has been the greatest gift of all

Thanks for reinforcing my positive attributes

I hold dear

all of the times we

One of my favorites is

You really boosted my spirits the day you called just to say

Life is

what we make it

so good I am with you.

You make my life complete by

San Diego, California
U.S.A.

Text by Maureen Webster

ISBN 0-7416-1313-1

www.havocpub.com

Made in Korea